Light Being

Foundations of Meditation
for Awakening Inner Energy

Peter Logos

Testimonials from Meditation Research

"**Short-term** meditation training **improves attention, self-regulation, and reduces anxiety**, depression, anger, fatigue, and stress-related cortisol levels." – *Proceedings of the National Academy of Sciences*, Yi-Yuan Tang et al. 1,490 citations, 2007.

"Mindfulness meditation produces demonstrable effects on brain and immune function, suggesting it may **change the brain** and **immune function in positive ways**." – *Psychosomatic Medicine*, R. Davidson et al., 2,845 citations, 2003.

"Mindfulness meditation has beneficial effects on **physical and mental health**, and **cognitive performance**." – *Nature Reviews Neuroscience*, Yi-Yuan Tang et al., 1,770 citations, 2015.

"Mindfulness **reduces emotional exhaustion** and **improves job satisfaction**." – *Journal of Applied Psychology*, Ute R. Hülsheger et al., 1,017 citations, 2013.

"Meditation increases **compassionate responding**, which may lead to more frequent acts to **relieve suffering of others**." – *Psychological Science*, P. Condon et al., 380 citations, 2013.

"Brief mindfulness training can enhance the ability to **sustain attention** and improve visuo-spatial processing, **working memory, and executive functioning**." – *Consciousness and Cognition*, F. Zeidan et al., 1,173 citations, 2010.

"Brief training in mindfulness meditation or somatic relaxation **reduces distress and improves positive mood** states." – *Annals of Behavioral Medicine*, Shamini Jain et al., 1,296 citations, 2007.

"**Meditation programs** can result in moderate reductions of multiple negative dimensions of psychological stress, **such as anxiety, depression, and pain**." – *JAMA Internal Medicine*, Madhav Goyal et al., 1,366 citations, 2014.

"Yoga has been shown to **improve children's executive functions**, including **focus, attention, and self-control**." *Science*, A. Diamond, et al. 2,388 citations, 2011.

"**Long-term meditators** self-induce sustained **high-amplitude gamma-wave** oscillations and phase-synchrony during meditation." – *Proceedings of the National Academy of Sciences*, A. Lutz et al., 1,117 citations, 2004.

"Mindfulness-based stress reduction is able to **reduce stress levels** in healthy people and **enhance spirituality values**." *Journal of Alternative and Complementary Medicine*, A. Chiesa et al., 1,567 citations, 2009.

Table of Contents

Cosmic Blessing Heart Prayer

We'll **start with a prayer** for the Earth and all sentient beings. You may substitute these words in a way that's appropriate to you.

"Heavenly Father, Divine Mother, Friend, Beloved God, Jesus Christ, great Masters and Saints of all traditions, **we bow in reverence** to you.

We humbly offer ourselves **in service, awakening to the universe** of higher consciousness **within each one of us.**

Let us be a source of light, to be kind, strong, wise, calm, and joyful, to bring about this **change within** ourselves, and in sharing this together, to change the world.

May all beings be happy and free."

Chapter 1 — Introduction to Meditation, The Monk and the Hot Dog Vendor

A monk was walking down the street in New York City. After a while, he started feeling hungry, so he decided to stop at the first place he saw—a **hot dog vendor.** The monk approached the vendor and said, **"Make me one with everything."**

The vendor prepared a hot dog, and the monk handed him a $20 bill. A minute later, the vendor gave the monk his hot dog, and the monk said, "Thank you very much." Then he asked, **"But where's my change?"** The vendor smiled and replied, **"Ah, change must come from within..."**

Thank you for joining and embarking on this meditation experience. As we explore and expand this opportunity to **experience life** with more depth, let's approach it **with a light heart**.

We'll be exploring the deeper natures of the self and our connection to the greater world around us as it relates to our own inner landscape and that experience of that dynamic interchange between **what is within us** and **what is outside of us**.

And to explore that, we'll look at how the world mirrors or shines a light on what exists inside us, and also being able to discern the deeper messages, **lessons and opportunities** that are present in every moment, with the goal of bringing more compassion, understanding, gratitude, forgiveness, and **joy to each moment**.

As we find our way through this practice, **wondering where to start** or wandering and pondering, let's remember to have fun. **Enjoy the process** of expanding your heart and mind, **making space for love in every moment** and interaction—not just for others, but for yourself. In these times, that is now more important than ever.

Remembering **to be kind and to love life**, to love the universe, to love whatever you feel in your heart to be true, and to see everything as something which can be brought into that experience of love, because we are nothing more than the expression of an infinite lineage of generations of information passed on.

It's only through **the care, attention, time and effort** of thousands or even **millions of generations** of people or proto-humans, even going all the way back to the **first single-celled organism** that we are here, sharing this moment together, and in the long arc of near-infinite time, **let's honor everything and everyone** that has allowed us to be here, and **make time for the timeless** here and now.

Have a wonderful day.

Chapter 2 — Concentration and Breath Awareness

Breath awareness offers us a simple way to begin a meditation practice **without needing** much theoretical or philosophical **ideas or information to fill our heads.**

Breathing fills up our hearts and in many ways this is more important for making initial progress. There was a team of **neuroscientists from Harvard** and they went to the Himalayas and studied with Tibetan Buddhist monks who'd been **practicing for 10,000 hours** or more. They pulled out their lab equipment and started putting electrodes on the monks' heads and the other **monks just started laughing** because they started **pointing to the heart.**

Connecting with the heart is where it all begins and there's been more information about yogis who can control their breathing to the point of being able to **control their heart rate at will.**

So for now, let's begin a **simple breath awareness practice**.

We'll start by sitting up nice and tall **connecting to a feeling of relaxation**, gratitude, presence in the moment for what is, whatever we happen to have experienced today or are **thinking about, and put that aside** for now, and allow ourselves to **be present with the experience of the breath.**

We can start to focus our awareness at the **sensation of breathing**, whether we feel it in the chest, in the nostrils, in the throat, in the belly, in the spine, making sure we're comfortable and relaxed and just starting to **tune in to this flow of energy**, flow of breath that's always happening, that's **already happening.**

Being aware of this process that's always happening **without our conscious effort** and yet how when we place our conscious attention on the breath to observe, to see, to notice if anything changes or how it changes.

We can feel the rising and falling of the chest or the gentle pressing in and out of the belly, the feeling of air flowing through the nostrils, **connecting to that space of your center** where you're not defined by your roles in the world, or by the tasks that you have to accomplish, by your philosophies or ideologies or moods, where just for even a moment, **you can be free from all of that** and experience the simple here and now **sensing the breath**, feeling this expansiveness of the breath **as it moves through you**.

You **become more aware** of the interchange of oxygen and carbon dioxide between the lungs and the heart, **pumping fresh, oxygenated blood throughout the entire body**.

Millions of red blood cells dying as millions more are being created in every moment, this **massive interchange of energy and bioelectricity in the body** that's all happening with some **innate intelligence** within us that medical science is aware of and yet hardly dares to explain beyond the understanding that, that is what **allows the body to heal.**

As we find this space **deeply nurturing**, if we do feel there's anything that needs healing that we offer an intention for that, for receiving the fullness of the breath and **the fullness of our concentration** or awareness on the breath and its ability to bring us new life, to **transform us into a higher energy state**, a higher version of ourselves without even changing the breath or doing a breathing exercise, simply by **placing our awareness on the breath**, we begin that journey.

We begin to experience the present moment free from our conditioning, **free to experience happiness, love, the surrender to transcendental bliss** that is always here when we're ready and willing to tap into it. Thank you.

Chapter 3 — Consistent Daily Practice

One of the first steps to making meditation a consistent part of daily life is to **carve out space and time every day** where you can make that a reality for yourself.

Most of us are at least to some degree **creatures of habit** and by performing **the same task, in the same place, at the same time** we ensure a greater level of coherence or consistency to our practice.

Whether it's in your bedroom or in another room, or if there's not the opportunity for you to practice inside your home, then outside on a porch, or **somewhere in open nature**. In time, at a busy intersection or in any environment you will be able to find that **centerpoint of stillness**.

For most people, practicing indoors, in your bedroom, is the **most consistent option**.

Many people find that sitting **before sunrise or after sunset** are the best times to sit but you figure out what works best for you.

If you have a **regular exercise** regimen in the morning, sitting for even 10 or 15 minutes **after exercising** or even hygiene like showering can be a great way to **link up a meditation practice with a routine that you already do.**

It's important to note that while you can meditate after eating, generally if you are also going to be sitting and practicing breathing exercises as well, it's good to have **some time in between eating and meditation**, two to three hours for a full meal, and if you are feeling a bit slow, go for a walk before you sit.

If you do decide to **meditate before eating,** then your meal will be extra relaxing, and as most of you know, **it's important to eat when you're feeling happy and relaxed** and not eat when you're feeling emotional. Eating with gratitude, in silence or in laughter, mindfully chewing your food, and sharing with others lets us bring the qualities of meditation into mealtime.

If we wish to find a deeper solution to emotional eating, practicing meditation before eating can be a great way to **digest any residual feelings from the day** or whatever else is going on by simply sitting, having a few deep breaths, and processing or least acknowledging anything that can wait, and returning more and more readily back to that state of health and joy.

As we reconnect to ourselves in these **moments between moments** in this timeless space that meditation can provide, finding consistency to practice doesn't have to be something that we necessarily share with anyone else, although having an **accountability partner** or a **group of people to practice with** or at least to support you in your practice can be a great way to **ensure that consistency**.

Chapter 4 — Three Deep Breaths

Three deep breaths is a simple reminder to **pause even for 30 seconds** when you are in-between moments.

Whether you are walking from one building to another and you find yourself about to **enter a room**, this can be a great opportunity to take three deep breaths whenever you are going to send an important message or **make an important call**.

It's a simple way to **retrain the mind, retrain the body** back into a state of connection to the practice of meditation, mindfulness and **heart connection**.

Three deep breaths is also a simple way to think about how to reconnect in that way, when there are so **many practices available to us, we don't need to over complicate it.**

We can simply remember that in these brief moments where we pause and focus on re-centering in whatever way we choose to, that three deep breaths is one of those ways to re-center and **prime the brain for success, relaxation, happiness,** joy and connection.

Finding what works for you, again, this is a simple tip, a simple reminder to **bring more of that daily practice into the rest of life.**

Chapter 5 — Breath, E-Motions, and Energy Control

"Use the Force you must." – Yoda

In yoga, there's a term called *pranayama*, which translates to **"control of the life force."**

Pranayama is also a word that's usually described as **breathing exercises**, although there's a greater context for pranayama, meaning **energy control,** for example, **physical, mental, and emotional regulation**.

Anytime we are feeling flustered or **emotional** in some way, we're sensing **e-motion as "energy in motion."**

As we connect to the breath, we can **create space and time to feel** how that **energy is moving through us** and actually begin to **control the**

way that energy moves, and how we respond to it.

To some degree, we allow that energy to take its natural course and **let the breath be the guide** for how that energy moves through the body, improving this **sense of intuitive intelligence.**

So "**breathing through feelings**" is one way of saying it, rather than simply suppressing or repressing feelings.

As we actually **feel what we're feeling** and are present to those feelings without needing to always outwardly express them at the same time, when we become aware of what's happening, we're **neither repressing or suppressing** negative emotion, we're feeling, breathing, and processing, so that those **emotions can be transformed and expressed in healthy ways that release pain and heal us,** rather than perpetuating illusions that we need to keep holding on to negativity out of convenience or familiarity, that **annihilating our pettiness and surrendering to the unknown** is actually where we meet our **greatest strengths.**

Usually a hurt can be felt, acknowledged, and **that emotion can then be released,** and we can become more skilled at repeating this practice with greater **clarity and catharsis** over time. Rather than only relying on external situations to change us, **we learn to take the driver's seat** and get where we need to, even if at times it's like racing Formula 1 with three wheels or a semi truck in Alaska, the **benefits of calmness and presence** continue to increase.

This is a **core principle, not unique to yoga and meditation**, but rather something that is common in many **modern psychological therapy** settings and **common sense.**

As we go through life, we invariably experience emotion and the opportunity to **transform emotion into something useful and beneficial** for our own sake of empowerment, and turning what one may see as a **challenge into an opportunity** for growth and letting go of heavy burdens, that this is an **overall attitude or mindset to approach life.**

A daily practice of meditation with understanding **what resistance is** or how we are experiencing the present moment as something that we can go deeper into, **especially when there is discomfort**.

We can, in many ways, **like a workout, experience a great catharsis** or a great release when we do **approach fear** or problems head on.

At the same time **being gentle and compassionate** with this process takes discernment and deep understanding of our own inner nature and that the more we practice, the more we find the **deep well of inner peace**, power, love, compassion, understanding, and forgiveness that is within us, we can begin to show that love **not just for our own inner critic,** but also for the other people around us, which **liberates** lots of of collective energy that's been **bound up in thinking a certain way.**

In understanding what breathing exercises can do for us, it's **not just about the health benefits or**

the surface layer inner peace, but it is about being able to move through life and ride the waves of life with grace, and knowing that this is something **we're all here to experience greater lessons and understanding** of why those lessons are here in the first place. **We have a toolkit like breathing exercises, like inner energy control.**

This mindfulness and meditation practice, that's shared by many traditions around the world, and now is **available to anyone to learn**, and it can give us a deeper level of resonance with truth, of **seeing beyond the veil** or reading between the lines in a situation of what needs to happen and **how to be of service**.

The practice of meditation gives us insight into all of the other areas of daily life for recognizing with **intuition** and a deeper level of **commitment** to our own awakening.

Chapter 6 — Breathing Exercise, Practicing Technique with Feeling

Breathing exercises often go hand-in-hand with meditation, and in some traditions, **breathing exercises will make up the majority of one's time spent in "meditation."**

There's a way of thinking about this as time spent with a technique and time spent without a technique in meditation, and oftentimes **the technique comes first and then "no technique" comes second.**

We have a series of things that we can do in order to **raise our energy, increase our focus, and open our heart** and bring ourselves into that space of inner connection or even inner communion, and that **once we're having an experience** or once we're feeling a depth within ourselves, space beyond the thinking mind, deeper relaxation, concentration, that **this is when we release the technique.**

If we are supposed to be doing 24 repetitions of a particular breath, and we find ourselves feeling very calm and relaxed and energized after only 12 or 15 rounds, then one doesn't need to continue with a technique for the sake of it being something that you were planning on doing, **once you're already having a deep experience you can relax and release the technique** and go into the practice of "no technique," focus on enjoyment in stillness.

For many of us, this is something that **comes with time** and this is **why techniques can be very beneficial** and why **breathing exercises are at the top of the list** of meditation techniques.

A simple breathing exercise we can practice is called **equal count breathing,** and equal count breathing takes a number of different forms.

One can say that **breathing in and out for the same amount of time** would consist of an equal count breathing exercise.

Two main forms of equal count breathing include *triangle breathing* (with a breath hold after the inhale) and *box breathing* (with a hold after inhale and exhale).

Box breathing is commonly known for being the same amount of time held in and out, so there's a breathhold after the inhale and after the exhale. It's all the same time count in seconds, for example **four in, four hold, four out, four hold, repeat.**

A **triangle breath** would simply minimize or **eliminate the breathhold after the exhale** in the box breath. This can be a little bit **easier than the box breath** and allow for a certain level of energy to move through the body when we're holding our breath with a full breath. This is like a standard breathhold.

Now before learning anything else, it's important to remember that we **relax when we're breathing,** that we're **not forcing the breath**, that we're doing our best to breathe diaphragmatically **rather** than with the chest muscles, **filling up the belly first** before filling up the chest with air.

We make sure that as we continue, we're staying relaxed and remembering to feel like we're more focused on **generating positive feeling**, love, positive energy than actually doing the technique.

The technique is important and in many ways it **is secondary to that feeling of love**, compassion, open-heartedness and **your reason why** you're doing this.

This reason can be **something big** like you're focusing on being of service to the planet, securing a business deal, or improving your connection to a deeper source or **spring of energy, kindness, and wisdom within** you.

Whatever the reason is, there's that space that you're giving yourself to receive a technique and to **fully embody** what it means and to understand that while breathing exercises by themselves even without any context can be incredibly beneficial when we do **connect the breath to a reason, to**

a why, we do it with feeling and when we practice a **technique with feeling** it brings us much closer to our goal.

The equal count breathing, triangle breath as a simple one **to start**, is simply breathing **in for four seconds, holding the breath for four seconds and exhaling for four seconds.**

Do this for a minute or two to start, **feeling how your energy changes** and then **sitting in stillness for a few minutes** after that. For a structure, repeat the breath for **three sets of six to twelve repetitions, twice a day.**

Chapter 7 — Preparing for Meditation, Internal-External World

Preparing for meditation doesn't require too much, although there's a few ways we can **increase our chances of initial success and repeated success**, and while success may be largely determined by you, one way of saying if something in meditation is successful is that you were able to repeat it and you were able to **notice something different about you** after the meditation.

Now, you may **not always have the same experience every time in the same way** that **when you go to the gym** when you practice consistently some days you may be sore or you may be feeling like you need more rest or you have a certain connection to the body in exercise or physical training that tells you **when it's important to rest and the times when you**

can push a little bit more and depending on your level of intensity and practice. Like the gym, **consistency is a prerequisite for intensity,** and it's better to get in a few minutes of practice every day and then **build your way up.**

Leading up to this, you'll have a greater sense of what that is, and for those of us who are starting off or **learning more about meditation** practice, then this is the opportunity to get reconnected or to reassociate with these **internal processes that are happening within us all the time.**

When we sense something as simple as **the body's natural relaxation response** or even the opening up to feelings of love and positivity that there's a process of opening up that we experience, and that over time we find ourselves in that space all the time, or that can be a goal that we see of being in a space of love that is beyond any external, or **a state of happiness that is beyond any external condition.**

When we think about **a result of meditation** that this bubbling joy, energy, or happiness that comes from the practice is one of those **hallmark keys** or cues, **bliss is given a high status,** because in many traditions it is seen as the **highest state** that with liberation, *nirvana*, ecstasy, these terms the **embodiment of bliss** is something that goes along with the practice of meditation.

The goal of meditation, is not the formal practice of meditation. In the long term, the goal of meditation is **a state that transcends any practice** that we are always in, or that it is a permanent state beyond all temporary states, which **spontaneously emerges from within us** once we let go of what's keeping us from experiencing that.

As we come into the practice of **preparing for meditation**, we can sense that we have a **physical environment** that we're preparing for ourselves, **a space to match our inner world.**

We have something like a **quiet, clean, calm space,** where we may have **candles** or **colorful items, soft blankets** or **pillows, pictures of people** that are inspiring to us like **saints or**

religious figures, or pictures that bring us **emotional resonance,** positive feeling or sacred **symbolism,** and finding a place where we can breathe **fresh air.**

Whether this space is somewhere with a **open window** to the outdoors, or at least making sure that **the air smells neutral** or we have an **air purifier using essential oils,** something like that, so that's the physical external environment.

With our inner environment, there's the **physiological environment of feeling loose and relaxed in the body,** feeling like if we do need to **practice yoga postures** or even **go for a walk or exercise,** or roll around the floor, or shake it out, or dance, or **wash your feet**, take a shower before meditation, these can all be **great ways to let go** of the internal processes in the body.

A little step deeper, is our **inner psychological, emotional, spiritual environment,** and as we tune into these deeper and deeper layers, we connect into ourself on a moment by moment basis, where all of that inner narrative of body, mind, thoughts and feeling, **becomes secondary to being**, being able to drop in and to **find our center regardless of what is going on** around us, what happens to be happening on the external, and even what happens to be happening internally.

The first phase would be to be calm when someone else is throwing a fit or something like that, to create space between our feeling and another's, and **the next phase** would be to remind ourselves when we're feeling that kind of way, then how we navigate and negotiate our own inner state and feeling and to create a certain **sense of "the witnessing self" to our inner experience.**

This **witness awareness** to thoughts and feeling, like the first phase, gives us a way to be **less attached, less identified,** where we are less caught up. We actually have a sense of **awareness of the feeling states that we're processing** as not our own, **emotions as visitors** that we **take responsibility for as temporary guests**.

We recognize that through breath, and through a deeper **sense of surrender**, and these deeper attitudes of gratitude, acceptance, and forgiveness, that we can prepare ourselves to go deeper regardless of whatever is happening around us or within us. At the same time, we see the value of working with direction, putting in effort to **live in a way that lets us be at peace within.**

While there is the simple process of **preparing a physical environment for meditation** which can very much influence the way we feel internally, if we do happen to be feeling some kind of way internally, whether physically or psychologically, that we have the mechanisms to prepare ourselves regardless of what's going on.

This **internal preparation** is important because **for maintaining a practice, we see the benefit** of it in navigating through all states of being, **surfing the waves** when they do come, **riding the highs and lows** of life.

We understand how we **become resilient** through a practice, so we **navigate all states with**

calmness and with practice, we reach this space where, like a good grandmother, we are closer to that **eternal state** of love, bliss, and happiness.

Chapter 8 — Abundance Meditation (8-8-8 Equal-Count Breath)

We'll be practicing an **equal count breathing** exercise.

This can be a **standalone practice** or something to **prepare for a sitting meditation.**

Start by finding a comfortable seat, making sure that you've **released any tension, letting go** of the day, any fidgety energy, turning off your phone, blowing your nose, drinking some water or tea, making sure you're warm, your environment is calm and peaceful, and that you have a little corner of quiet space.

Fresh air like an open window is ideal.

Now for this breathing exercise, we'll be practicing nostril breathing, **breathing through the nose.**

However, if you are experiencing any obstruction, then you're more than welcome to **breathe through the mouth.**

We'll be breathing *diaphragmatically* as best as we can, so **breathing into the lower belly**, filling up the abdomen area **between the belly button and the spine,** and then filling the chest after that.

This is an **inhale, hold, exhale.**

We're feeling the **energy** that's moving on the breath, **moving through the body**, so doing your best to do this with relaxation, **never forcing the breath,** feeling a deeper sense of connection to yourself and to that space of the timeless within you.

We'll start by expelling the breath with an exhale, **breathing out gently** and starting our **inhale for a count of eight**, breathing in, and **holding the breath for eight, and exhaling for eight,** releasing all the air here as **smooth and even** as you can.

Breathing in for eight, filling the lungs, holding the breath for eight, and exhaling for eight **relaxing the lungs.**

For **ten more repetitions of 8-8-8 (12 total breaths)**, inhaling, holding the breath, and exhaling.

For the last breath, inhaling with feeling, **sending energy through the whole body** on this last inhale, holding the breath, and releasing, **letting go of this breath technique**.

Now after these 12 breaths, hold the breath out without forcing, and be as still as you can, **until you are ready to take a breath in**, and see how it feels to **not immediately take a breath in,** but if you do feel the need to catch your breath, then by all means, please do so.

Returning back to your natural flow of breathing, connecting to that space of calmness and centeredness within yourself, feeling this **regulation of energy, the electrical currents** traveling through the nervous system, being **soothed by the breath.**

Sitting still, we feel this **energetic shift within us** towards a state of deeper calmness, presence, joy, and relaxation. Do you best **bring this feeling with you** through the rest of your activities and interactions.

Chapter 9 — Body Scan Relaxation (Yoga Nidra/Nap Time)

In yoga practice, **the final resting pose**, *savasana*, **laying flat on your back**, is **the most important pose** because it is where we receive the benefits of any other postures. It's where we practice **total surrender, total relaxation, regeneration and bliss.**

Similarly, **with strength training**, the body doesn't start synthesizing protein, **building muscle until you are sleeping.**

Laying flat on the back, not coincidentally, is said to be **the best way to sleep** because it allows for **the spine to decompress** and **the organs to detoxify** without being squished.

Practicing laying on the back for **a few minutes at a time** helps to work your way up to sleeping like this, and **pillows and blankets** are encouraged.

Yoga nidra is a like a **power nap**, with the practice of savasana as a way to recharge during the day, with the key difference being you **do your best to be as relaxed as possible while staying awake**, it's normal to fall asleep.

The **body scan** is the practice of **entering deep relaxation** in yoga nidra or before **meditation or bedtime**, but can be used as an awareness practice anytime.

As we **relax into the body scan**, either sitting or laying on the back, gently release any leftover tension that you still have by **inhaling, tensing and holding the entire body,** and then **exhaling, relaxing and feeling the entire body.**

You can try this two more times.

Inhale, tense the body completely, then exhale, fully relaxing the body.

Last time, inhale, tense, exhale, release the entire body.

Now find your natural rhythm, **natural flow of breath**, so you start to release into deeper and **deeper layers of relaxation**.

We'll start moving from **the toes all the way up to the top of the head**, relaxing progressively as we go.

Focus on sending the breath and **energy throughout the entire body** as we practice.

First, releasing the muscles of **each toe**, the bottoms of the feet, ankles, and heels, **sending deep breaths**, and releasing the legs, the calves, the thighs, the knees, releasing **the hips** and the groin, **the lower back**, sacrum, releasing the entire spine, moving **one vertebrae at a time** as you relax deeper and deeper, releasing the muscles, **the hands**, fingertips, palms, wrists, forearms, elbows, biceps, and shoulders, all releasing completely, relaxing the muscles of the abdomen, the chest, **the heart, opening these spaces up to new life**, releasing the muscles of the throat, **the neck**, the chin, and the jaw, finally relaxing the muscles of the face, **the eyes**, the mouth, ears, the nose, **with a smile**, even the top of the head.

As you focus on bringing new, fresh life, **fresh energy** into the body, relax and feel your body expanding with golden, **radiant light from within.**

As this light grows, **you feel lighter and lighter** until you dissolve into the fabric of the universe.

Chapter 10 — Be You, Choose Your Destiny

This is a reminder that **being yourself** is important to remember, and **you can decide** who you want to be all the time. There's no fixed identity based on the outer world.

You have your **traits of your personality** and these different characteristics or components that make you up. At **the core of that is you**.

You are an individual. There's no question about that. You are already you, so you don't really have to do anything else other than **listen and act from that center**.

It's about not trying to be anything other than you, letting go of all of that, and being able to experience yourself, **being okay with you as you are**, being at peace with you, and the more that you're at peace with yourself, the easier it is to be yourself.

And at the same time, just be at peace with yourself now, remembering that "love is an act of eternal forgiveness" and "action is the antidote" to worry.

When there's any doubt or question that you have in your mind about who you are, cast it aside, and **affirm who you are by taking action** towards the things that you feel and reason to be the most urgent and important to you.

These bring you to your highest self, into your heart, into your **connection to aliveness and exuberance**.

As you get better at tuning into that, you will **experience more of who you are.**

You'll start to recognize there's **this thread in everyone that connects us all**, every single one of us.

When we start to see that interconnectedness, there is this, "infinite I" or this **"eternal you"** however you want to say that, that exists in all of us, and that **we are sharing that experience**, it starts to become about understanding that expressing yourself or being yourself is the thing that **everybody is here to do** — and there's this **core of individuality** that is central to our experience of **life satisfaction**.

It's important **for people to feel like their mind and soul are capable** of expressing itself and that being in this world is often a place where, you know, we are repeatedly reminded, to put it gently, that **things are a certain way here on Earth**, and being able to understand that is a part of reality and still being able to be yourself is the challenge, **the obstacle transforming into opportunity.**

That's **why we gather together and why we have these practices**. We are interested in learning more about **shaping and sharing our inner realm**, and being able to **tap into** meditation practices and creativity, and being able to discover more about **how we respond** to the things in our environment that **inspire us** or bring us more joy, the like activities or the events that you enjoy with the people around you and the things that speak to you.

How you **incorporate ideals into your life** so that you are experiencing **the fullness and the variety** whether they're experiences that you want to have externally or qualities that you want to **cultivate within** yourself, whether it's, "I want to have a dinner party with my friends" or "I want to cultivate better writing skills," or" I want to cultivate more inner peace or wisdom," you can approach it at any level small to big, **surface level to deep**, and you're still coming from this **place of heart**, that is the book, and **you choose how to write the story of your life.**

This is the life that **we all are given**, and we are here to experience and to write our stories. I encourage you to get ready to **tell yours the way no one else can.** That's what being yourself is all about.

Chapter 11 — Self-Realization, Yogananda, and Kriya Yoga

Connecting to **everything that we are** and everything that we can be is something that we would call a process of **self-realization or self-actualization**.

This has been examined through the lens of **modern psychology** as something in modern **medical science** that has actually drawn from many of the **Eastern wisdom** traditions throughout the ages.

Yogananda is one of the yogis who originally brought yoga to the West and formed Self-Realization Fellowship headquartered in Hollywood, and over the last hundred years has made a great impact on millions around the world through the merging of the practices of combining modern **neuroscience with meditation**, a deeper understanding of psychology, and the **unity in world's religions**, in particular, Hinduism and Christianity.

Yogananda himself got a degree in psychology in order to be able to bridge all of the teachings that he received in India with the modern Western interpretations of the **mind and human behavior.**

There's a great lineage of teaching that he draws upon, which is called **Kriya yoga**, which is not unique to Yogananda, but it is a lineage that has been carried and began to be brought back from the ancient yogis about 200 years ago.

Kriya is a science of inner transformation that was held secretly for hundreds of years, because essentially humankind was not ready, until we reached **this stage of psychological, inner evolution** as well as the **industrial-technological revolution** that has led to the **interconnectedness of our planet** with supply chains and the internet that has never been seen before.

Now at this time of great energetic transformation of the planet, **the yogis have made these teachings available,** so that we, **the average person** or the Western man or woman with dedication, can evolve into a higher **state of mind** or consciousness.

If you are interested in learning more about that, the first book to read is Yogananda's ***Autobiography of a Yogi,*** which Steve Jobs, the founder of Apple computers, kept as the only book on his iPad, the book that he recommended at his Stanford commencement speech, the last public speech he ever gave, where he left a copy at everyone's seat. This speaks to one person's experience with that book, something that Jobs would read every year.

Autobiography of a Yogi gives an **East meets West** account of many unique individuals, of the connection between **perception and perspective**, and different ways of looking at the world. If you've never been to India or the East, and you live somewhere in the Western world, that there's many ways of seeing things, **doors you will learn how to open**, which can lead to significant changes in your life and the world around us.

Feeling the **depth of our interconnectedness through another's perspective** can be a window to our own evolution. This is a reminder to remember the **deeper reasons** for meditation, **beyond relaxation or concentration**, and yet **those are the first steps** to waking up to the love in **your heart**, and we're all in it together. Thank you for being open to considering new ideas.

Chapter 12 — Plato's Allegory of the Cave

The simple story of Plato's *Allegory of the Cave*, is over 2,000 years old from ancient Greece, and resonates as being especially relevant for modern times. The premise or the setup is that there are two groups of people, the first are prisoners, who are **sitting in a cave** facing the back wall of the cave, opposite the entrance.

Behind these people closer to the entrance, there's **a large fire**, and behind the fire, there are the second group, the guards, people who are making **shadow puppet figures** and displaying them through the fire, so that the people who are imprisoned see **shadows on the wall**.

The people who are facing the wall, who don't turn around to see those who are making the shadows against the wall, these people **believe that the shadows being flickered on the wall are reality,** that whatever stories are being portrayed **represent the truth**.

One prisoner, known as "the Philosopher," figures out how to **escape and exits the cave**, wanders out into the sunlight and sees the light of the sun and sees the trees and sees a beautiful meadow and is **utterly amazed** by what he sees. This person represents anyone searching for truth or deeper meaning.

In recognizing this reality, which he has **never experienced before**, and yet can't help but feel that this is a **much more real reality than the shadow figures** being flickered on the wall. Upon recognizing this, this free individual then **goes**

back into the cave to tell the people about the world outside.

When the free man enters back into the cave, because it's so dark in there and he's been in the sun, **he's temporarily blind**. And so, what this person discovers when they go back into the cave and **start to tell the people who are staring at the wall** what is going on in **the beautiful world outside the cave,** they don't believe him, because he is blind in the cave, and they take this to mean the world outside the cave is dangerous, and go back to accepting the world of shadow puppetry. The quest of this person who is free, is to **recognize the situation and act accordingly.**

In many ways this story has a great number of **metaphorical and psychological representations within ourselves**, it's not just about people who are manipulative or trying to keep other people in the dark, and that there are a few who have gone into the light and some of those have come back to free the others.

This story is something happening *within* all of us, we can say there's patterns of seeking out the shadow games for a sense of comfort and that the **shadows representing a static known reality** and yet only being abstractions of an abstraction, that someone else has presented knowingly or unknowingly, being something that we have yet to realize, is only a projection.

As Carl Jung says, "beware of unearned wisdom." As we recognize shadows for being shadows, and step into the brilliant warm beautiful light of the sun, and bask in its rays, the only way to **describe what it's like** is as if you have never tasted an orange and you're describing to someone **what an orange tastes like.**

If you have a **direct experience**, you can relate that direct experience to someone else who has had it and yet in communicating that with someone who has not had the same experience, there's a great level of connection required to translate that to a first-hand experience. Like the Buddha says, "I am not the moon, but I can point my finger to it." **Shoot for the moon, friend.**

The question of **"how much of our lives we are experiencing through abstraction,"** taking the word of others, or taking for that second-hand experience, that we have a certain level of trust and discernment, that we can employ to the best of our ability to get good information on whatever we want to learn about ,and that that's a smart thing to do, that learning from others is incredibly valuable, and yet it is **no substitute for direct experience**, or primary reference.

One of the best things that anyone can give from that place of expertise or advice is to bring one into that place of **being able to have their own experience**. If in the process of communicating that, one has some kind of experience, then it's only a sign that a true direct experience goes beyond all words or knowledge.

Metanoia is a Greek word, meaning **"experiencing the transcendental,"** that there's a great peaceful or blissful or indescribable experience, beyond what we would normally think of as being a human being.

It's through feeling that we come into that space of knowing who we are or knowing what we are knowing what the truth is beyond what anyone has told us, and still referencing what anyone tells us with our own experience, so that we can say, **"ah, I**

have tasted the orange, but you know where the orange tree is." Like stepping into the sunshine for only a second, that first moment of bringing that light into the cave of our awareness, and in bringing ourselves into this experience **there's no limit** to what we can experience once we have stepped out of the cave.

The funny thing of course which can be said now, is that in the modern world, many of us spend time indoor **modern cave dwellings**, looking at **flickering screen objects**, which have very flattering light shadows appearing on them. At some point we go step outside into the bright brilliant sunlight and see what a beautiful world there is to behold in say the beauty of a forest, a park, a river, the ocean, or the mountains, and so the literal translation or interpretation of this story, which again comes from over 2,000 years ago from ancient Greece, connects us back into this space that's stretching across space and time, to where we are now in the most peculiar way.

For the reason of reminding us to go outside, not because that's what philosophers do, but because anyone who enjoys life recognizes that there's more to experience than beyond the four walls of a living space, or **beyond the so-called four walls of our own thinking mind.**

While expanding our thinking process is a wonderful thing to do, and **increasing our ability to articulate, learn, and express** the deeper experiences that we have, that that's simply an afterthought or a reflection of the depth to which we have or can experience, that which we cannot describe in words.

The joy and the beauty and the love and the truth of this world in some ways we can **never speak of**, there's always something that remains beyond expression, and that that's something that we can savor, that you may **share with others through a smile** or a glimmer in your eyes.

By tracing this thread that runs through each of us, we can begin to **set each other free**, to release from the ideas or **spells that we've placed upon ourselves,** that this world is much bigger than any of us can really know, even if we picture walking across **all the corners of the Earth,** there's always some wild part of the earth that will never be fully explored at least by any one of us. When **we sit in quietness** even in our own room, the world as we think of it falls away and a space emerges with patience and relaxation where we experience this inner sun, **the light of awareness.**

As this awareness and perception grow, we bring it with us similarly to the light of the sun that as if we could bring the light of the sun into the cave, just to show someone **a droplet of sunlight, of loving awareness,** and its infinite brightness compared to any flame, or to any shadow, that the brightness of the sun dispels all shadows, and it's only when we're looking away from the sun that we do see a shadow.

In reflecting on our own practice, and our process of integrating the subconscious mind with the conscious mind, or even what we'd call the **"super-conscious mind"** or that light, that brilliance that we all experience in certain moments, where we go beyond what we think of as our own abilities, that we're somehow connected to the universe.

We have this **galactic intelligence within in our DNA**, we can command that strength and light and power to flow through us, to bring ourselves into that state, into that place that is already present within us, and that we get to **recognize and remember.**

It's more about **enjoying that light of the sun,** enjoying that brilliance and the breeze in the trees, and **fully experiencing that,** which then allows us to **share with others.**

Chapter 13 — Guided Experience (Coming Home, Returning to Essence)

When we imagine time and space as a medium for physical existence, **the same way that a fish is swimming in water,** we are swimming in a **soup of vibrations** that we're not always completely entirely aware of, until we change the **qualities and dynamics of space-time** itself through something like **sound and music.**

When we **generate sound from within,** with humming, chanting, or singing, we **become that element of sound** within ourselves, and that **changes our biology**, our essence to the frequency or vibration that we're singing.

This is **why the kind of music we listen to** is very important, to choose good quality music, good quality sounds, good quality audio files, to be in tune with the **resonant frequencies** all around us, not just sound, but all kinds of vibrations.

To generate that frequency, **the vibration within us influences the environment** around us, to be in harmony and frequency with that orchestra of symbiotic connection that **we share as all being musical notes in this larger universal symphony.**

When you recognize this dance that we're moving through in space-time, we find ourselves connected to that song and that beat and **that feeling that we vibe with when we're feeling true in ourselves.**

This makes us **more aware of what freedom is**, or how to become closer to that.

The expression of individuality in the service to something larger, in the connection and **experience of something larger than oneself**, to share something bigger than oneself, is the feeling, **the memory**, the experience of **the universe within you.**

We are all mirrors, to share and **shine our light to each other.**

Everybody gets a different spectrum of **the rainbow**, and together we all shine with that prism, the **full color spectrum** of light that we are.

This gives life richness and variety, a feeling of **the ability to blend in by standing out**, the freedom to be yourself, **to not be afraid** of being whoever you are, **to connect to that essence** within you that calls to be expressed in some way, shape, or form.

Letting your energy, your life, your vibrations, **be an offering** to something beyond you, to love, **to the collective happiness** of all people, to **the freedom and empowerment of all people.**

To be able to **live from one's center**, and be in connection to that **as we move throughout the storms** that life may throw our way, only to come out **smiling when the sun returns.**

As we connect deep within, **the strength of our core** and our center, this bright light within us, we find that **radiant essence within everyone** around us.

That **as we connect that within** ourselves, connecting to that deeper, we connect deeper to others, and **we give others the opportunity** to connect to that within themselves.

We feel ourselves relaxing into **the meaning of feeling.**

Tuning into the experience of here and now, **whatever presents itself** without giving extra thought to the thought.

To **observe thought, without judgment**.

To bring focus to the breath, finding the **flow of breath**, long, smooth, and relaxed.

Connecting to the spine, **feeling strong, stable, supported.**

Allowing for pauses in the breath to notice those **moments of breathlessness in between** the inhale and the exhale.

Tuning into **the heartbeat**.

Connecting to **the rhythm** of the heart.

Releasing, **letting go** of any tension as you exhale.

Inhaling in fresh energy, **life force**, strengthening, exhaling, letting go.

Purifying, releasing.

Finding that natural flow, cycling this energy, **generating new energy** with the inhale and **recycling anything** that needs to be recycled.

Return back, to be **rebirthed from the ashes**, renewed, refreshed, regenerated, **restored**, beyond original condition, transmuted into a new alchemical form, **the phoenix**.

Finding that space within you, to take flight to your true feeling, your true heart, **soaring with that confidence of love, the strength of heart.**

That power, innate in every single one of us.

To be free. To be **together in that freedom.**

Sharing the joy. **Filling all hearts.**

As we look to the stars and the celestial abodes, the planets and **the moon, the sun**, we see ourselves as small.

Finding our place in the universe allows us to see something within ourselves, that we are reflected in the galaxy of experience that one human is.

And as we recognize that **each person is a walking galaxy** of love and wisdom.

We can bring our heart to experience each moment with a greater **sense of connection**.

A greater curiosity to **explore the everyday and the ordinary moments** in life that we share can become a transcendental doorway.

Shared in the conversation while in the grocery checkout line, or while doing the laundry.

And as you **find that dimension** experienced throughout your daily life.

It generates and it grows and it activates, and it **brings more clarity** to a world that is ready.

Finding space in between moments to breathe, look at the sky, see the birds and remember to **sing your song, walk your talk, live your dream.** Peace.

Lokah samastah sukhino bhavantu. (**May all beings be happy and free.**) Om. Om. Om.

Chapter 14 — Entering Flow State (in the Yin-Yang of Life)

The science of **heart rate variability (HRV) training** shows that we can tune into the rhythms of our heart by being aware of the cadence, obviously, and it's not just about our heart rate, but the subtle rhythms over time can show us when we're more in need of rest or exercise – and our **ability to focus and handle and manage stress** can all be measured within the heart.

As we come into this space of deeper **awareness around our state of being**, we can understand that flow is really a multi-dimensional experience within ourselves of becoming the full-fledged human being that we are all born and here created to be.

When we understand the depth of being able to **tune into our heart** and to understand that we have these two different flows within ourselves, we have the, let's just say the polarities that make up the **non-duality**.

This polarity makes up the enmeshment of these two principles of light and dark, **yin and yang**, *Shiva and Shakti*, **the masculine and feminine**, fire and water, **movement and rest**, these creative principles at play within each person.

We have the ability to understand, through this law of polarity, that we have our **sympathetic** and **parasympathetic nervous system,** working together.

We have this **"rest and digest"** and the **"fight, flight or freeze,"** in neuroscience terms these days, there's different ways of naming the two systems, but essentially it's like you have your **awake and alert** and then you're **relaxed and resting**.

There's **activities that complement each** of those states.

So we have **any form of exertion**, whether that's building a house, or going on a run, or studying for an exam, or giving a speech, anything that requires a **moderate amount of energy and focus.** This is that flow that we normally think about.

It's also what we think about **when we imagine surfing or skydiving or skiing**, some kind of extreme sports, is that kind of super intense flow.

If that was the only kind of flow, we'd be missing out on a lot of everyday experiences, that can be just as blissful and more nourishing on **the other end of the spectrum of flow**.

Those are all the experiences associated with **meditation practice** that are geared toward **recovery and regeneration** and building the body, **the vital essence back to its original homeostasis**, and that's our beginning place where we can start to experience, for a lot of people, a different kind of release or relaxation. In a world, where we are so common to **"go, go, go"** then burn out in Western culture, this ever-refreshing way of existence, actually lets us be **more productive with more energy in less time.**

Flow states are important **for the everyday workforce.** There's a lot to be said for actual **productivity in the workplace**, being higher when people are in flow, and the fact that 80% of a lot of work days are just being caught up in bureaucratic minutiae, or whatever happens to be the flavor of the day, there is a **high economic and cognitive cost of attentional switching,** and **the highest rewards** emerge from flow state.

It's important to remember that regardless, **our duties are here to serve us** and we are not here for them, in the sense that we work for things that are important that must be done, and that those things can be done in flow with greater **satisfaction and effectiveness**.

Building flow within us, letting **meditation flow into "productive time,"** builds our connection to our breath, our connection to our community, and to the divine and to the miracle of life, leading to **success in business and creative expression**.

The things that inspire us, when we really start to live and **embody and embrace** that within ourselves, the flow naturally comes, and there's ways of **coaxing the flow**.

That's what most people are thinking about, **"how you enter flow state,"** it's about **recognizing it's already here**, it's not something that you even achieve, rather than an **attitude of willingness** you surrender to, in the sense of you're recognizing that **there's a river and you can go swimming in it**.

It's as simple as that, and that enjoying the adventure of flow, is part of the bliss of that journey. Making the practice of **being in tune with the frequency of your own inner nature** and *interoception*, is a simple way of remembering you have the internal perception, **inner sight**.

The **awareness of your physical body** in space is *proprioception*, this is a three-dimensional sense of the body in space, and *interoception* is **how are you feeling inside**, like what's going on, like what's going on with your stomach, what's going on with your muscles, or your emotions or **energy in the body**, what is going on in your mind, that's the interoceptive realm.

So there's a lot to be said for interoception, the **self-awareness** of tuning into the feeling of "there's an **entire being in here** to explore, that we didn't necessarily **receive the user manual** to."

One of the **quickest ways** to dial into this **internal supercomputer** is flow, a spark of the same frequency generating the creation of the universe. We have breath, and **breath is a direct interface**, and then we have our heart, like the power of our **heart, the power of pure feeling**, the ultimate unconditional love, the bliss of that divine love, that we can feel in our hearts every day.

We grow in our hearts, and **we pour out with abundance** because love is infinite and it's lovely knowing that the flow of love is an **infinite**

resource. I wish for you to experience that flow in your own life, to **follow the breath, listen to your heart, and enjoy every moment**.

Chapter 15 — Heart Coherence (HRV) Guided Meditation

We will be going over a simple HRV guided practice. This is about bringing our **heart into a state of coherence with our brain** and using our breath to accomplish this.

Now, if you've never practiced meditation or breathing exercises or anything like that, the simplest thing to know is to **keep breath smooth and even to stay relaxed**, use your belly, keep your belly relaxed.

It's okay to **let your belly stick out when you inhale**, don't draw your belly in when you inhale, feel it relax and expand, feel your **diaphragm in that concave area below your rib cage**, expand and contract the diaphragm is actually one of the **key muscles** for our breathing.

And it mostly is about drawing air into that lower abdominal region.

As we get better at that, it helps us **release a lot of stagnant energy** and it helps us take deeper, fuller breaths when we are doing a breathing exercise.

Focusing on using your belly to breathe and staying relaxed as you practice, breathing through the nose into the belly, feeling that connection **halfway between, in the heart**.

As we inhale up, feel like you're filling up your belly with like **a vessel that's filling up with water, from the bottom up,** in the same way your belly is filling up with air.

And then as you **breathe this energy up**, it's like the level is filling up and then we're exhaling and that water level, emptying from the chest and then finally the lower belly.

Take a few minutes to read through this and then you can go on to continue in silence at your own need.

Sit up tall, find your **gravitational center**.

Find that balance point where your posture is perfectly even, where **you are supported by the bones of your spine** so that your muscles surrounding your spine **work as minimally as possible** for you to sit up as straight as you are able.

And then from there, let's **relax our shoulders**.

Roll the shoulders back once or twice and squeeze the shoulder blades together just a little bit to open the heart.

As you do this, you can practice an inhale as you **squeeze the shoulder blades** back and together.

Feel like the heart is opening as you practice, keeping an **even pace of the inhale and the exhale.** We'll focus on this energy in our heart, breathing in a way so that we are expanding the heart.

You can focus even on expanding the space, literally and physically with the lungs, and **expanding this area of the lungs**.

As we tune into our nervous system, we can **use our hands** as a metric.

Here's an exercise to connect the movement of the hands with the in and out breath, to **improve the smoothness and flow of the breath**. With hands close together at your waist level, breath in with arms reaching forward, raise the hands all the way up along the centerline of the body, to in front of the head with arms outstretched, then bringing the hands closer to the face and exhaling while lowering the hands along the centerline again, this time closer to the front of the body, back down to the waist, **making a circular motion. Breath in as you raise the hands, breath out as your lower the hands**. Continue this breathing pattern with the hands for a few repetitions, as often as needed.

This is a simple way to **connect the energy of the hands to the heart,** and the hands are connected to the heart directly when you look at the nervous system.

The **hands serve as an extension of the heart** in some ways.

So you're bringing the loop back in on itself, creating an infinity loop, **cycling a wheel** of breath energy within the body.

This **wheel of energy** is actually really potent for releasing tension in the nervous system which can cause an over-activated sympathetic nervous system. We use this to activate the **parasympathetic nervous system**.

Then, **place your hands on your chest** or your sternum. As you're breathing, breathing into the heart, if there's anywhere that you feel in particular to breathe into, you can place your hands there and just feel that area expanding.

As you breathe into this **center point in your heart**, you can start to tune into that cycle of the breath, of the inhale and the exhale, the energy of the sympathetic of the "take action" nervous system, and then the "rest rejuvenation" of the parasympathetic nervous system.

We're inhaling, exhaling. You can use a pace of about four seconds each, in and out, to start. You can always increase to a level that's right for you, remembering to **use the diaphragmatic breath** and keep the hands on the chest if you like.

As you inhale, you **fill up the diaphragm**, the belly and then the chest using that cue of filling up completely from the belly up and then using the **hands on the heart to open the heart** a little bit more.

Doing your best to keep the rhythm of this breath smooth and even once again. It's just like we are in the sea on a boat and we're **traveling over the crest of the wave and then the trough of the wave.**

You're expanding and releasing, feeling that expansion, release. Letting go, **bringing in the new.** You can keep going at your own pace for a few more rounds.

Connect deep within, find that space in the heart, **feel the heart expanding** and opening as you practice this, continue your natural breathing when you're ready. Thank you for practicing.

Chapter 16 — Embodiment of a Mindset

In yoga philosophy, **yoga postures and meditation are often connected** and combined so that meditation usually follows after the postures.

Originally, postures were less emphasized, it was more that **breathing exercises and meditation were connected**.

In the modern world, there's all numbers and kinds of different practices that we can do for embodiment or for relaxation or for health or fitness or for inner development, so offering a **tradition rooted in hatha yoga** and meditation is one way to bridge this mind-body connection.

We can say that mind and body really are the same thing, that when we practice something, any kind of embodiment practice, we are **embodying a state of consciousness,** or a state of being, and that that state is felt not just in the brain, or in the mind, as somehow disconnected from the body, but in fact **in the body** is where we experience this.

When we do **go into meditation**, we've **brought up these feelings of love and joy** and connection **through embodiment**, then in many ways it makes it much easier to let go of the body and to release the bodily consciousness so that we can **be in stillness** and release any of that residual tension.

Embodiment practices like hatha yoga postures serve as a vehicle for connecting us back into the body in a way where we remember that we are not the body and yet the body is a vehicle for bringing us into a higher state of consciousness.

This is one way of looking at it, where we can have a very deep and intimate and delightful connection to a practice that allows us to be **connected to the body and yet free from it**.

Feeling your way into this, I mentioned the yoga postures that would lead up to a meditation practice, and any number of other **martial arts or calming physical exercises that can be beneficial** as well.

Making sure that we are **exercising with attention and with concentration** and with awareness of that idea of bringing energy into the body or of focusing on the individual muscles or of **bringing more joy into the body** when we do anything and recognizing how that sort of happening in the body makes life a little bit more fun.

I would recommend that you find what works for you even if it's something as simple as **dancing or shaking your arms and legs, jumping up and down, going for a walk,** all these kinds of things can bring a lot of benefit to life and to practice.

Chapter 17 — Principles of Inner Energy

Inner energy moves through us and we are capable of becoming aware of how this energy moves and then how to move this energy, and there's **deeper layers of energy** and more obvious **surface layers of energy**.

If I were to say **clench your fist and squeeze,** you'd be working with a surface layer level of physical energy, and at the same time you'd be aware that the **command for your brain** to send to your hand of "clench and make a fist" requires a more **subtle layer of thought energy** in order to make that happen.

If we are aware of how **thought influences the energy**, and then how the energy then influences the physical form, we can in turn **redirect the flow of energy** within ourselves to bring about a change of consciousness, a change of state, a change of mind, a change of being and a **simple**

principle like tensing muscles and releasing them can actually connect us to this **deeper source of willpower** that is required to move energy through the body.

There's a certain set of exercises that **Paramahansa Yogananda** developed that's called **Energization exercises,** they're like many other **isometric exercises** similar to even what **modern weightlifting** emulates, only that you're not using weights, and it's a unique practice to the world of yoga.

Energization is a practice that connects us to actual **bodybuilding** and even more, **energy building,** that there's a way to build up the physical body so that the physical body is strong and muscley, and there is also the deeper layer of building up the **energy body**.

Oftentimes people can be strong and muscley and you wonder if are they fully energetic, and some people can be leaner and also the same question is if they are energetic, so the **ability to work with whatever condition the body is in,** and be able to bring more energy into the body is a way of connecting us to our deeper **source of willpower**, which one could say is a way of **strengthening the thought**, or the consciousness, of one's own self and without strengthening the ego.

We're focusing on **strengthening the pure dynamic energy** of the body which is free from the ebbs and flows of circumstance and as we connect into that layer of energy in the body we become more capable of performing tasks that are required of us, and doing those tasks with more joy and energy.

As we connect to the principle of inner energy we see that we could even call it **"mental kung fu"** or something like that, where there's a lot that is going on inside of us, and when we see something that's representative on the outside of something like being able to do a push-up for example, where **there's a lot that has to happen internally in order to be able to do a push-up.**

As most of us know, it's about **being willing** to do an exercise, and a big part of that is seeing yourself successfully performing it. As we reconnect to **willpower, as central to energy,** then strengthening willpower and **having the means or tools** for strengthening willpower can be valuable, if not central, to the whole practice of meditation, **raising our energy to superhuman levels.**

The willingness, and **the attitude of willingness** in many ways is that **first step,** and this is simply one suggestion, or one way of going about it. The **energization exercises from Yogananda** which generally are isometrics for tensing and releasing the body, and bringing that awareness of energy in the body, is one way to do that.

Any way that you go about bringing more energy into the body, through the conscious use of **willpower yields beneficial results**. Whether you're lifting weights or doing some other kind of exercise, they can all be done with that principle of awareness of bringing more energy into the body, so that one, you're not overextending yourself, and two, you're **doing it with a reason.**

You're going to have many reasons for doing practice when you know there's **health and fitness benefits**, there's sheer looks, there's reaching a certain goal that you want to achieve, there's competition, and then there's that principle of raising our consciousness or even improving our mood. As we dive into that principle of energy, we can feel that **the outer principle and the inner principle really are connected** and that as we start to work with that that energy, **we notice results.**

Chapter 18 — Yoga Postures (Asana), Stillness, and Dancing

Asana as a practice of embodiment, in many ways more so than other physical practices, brings us to the awareness of cultivating states of consciousness through a physical movement or **practice of movement and stillness.**

And we can be **strengthening the mind while strengthening the body.**

And this is not unique to yoga, in that many **sports psychologists and coaches know** that this is what's happening.

The mind is a muscle and we're training the mind when we're training the body. As we practice we can **cultivate a state of being that goes beyond** anything physical.

At the same time, knowing **what to practice and how to practice** makes a big difference.

As we find **what works for us**, simple practices with **fewer postures per session**, brings more clarity, and lets us focus more on reaching a **depth of each posture**.

We can treat poses like exercise or as a workout and this is how yoga is practiced in modern time. Finding that level of **stillness in a single posture** can be incredibly challenging to find the depth and ability to continue to breathe through one posture when we are holding it, **working to defy gravity**.

There's a saying that goes back as early as the beginnings of yoga, **"the perfection** of a single yoga posture is when you can **hold it for three hours straight** without moving."

So there's an incredible amount of strength that's required to **hold a position like a statue** and focusing on breathing while in a posture brings us a different kind of awareness rather than always moving from one posture to the next to the next to the next.

That being said, there's a place for **flowing movement** and a place for fitness and a place for **the wild swirling energy** that is within you and even the first yogi *Shiva,* as it goes by legend, sat in meditation like a stone for many many hours or even days, and then upon rising from this long period of meditation, had brought up so much **bliss and ecstasy,** that all he could when he got up was do was dance and dance and **dance and dance and dance.**

In connecting to that principle of the yin yang of **movement and stillness,** we connect to that principle of bliss, and that principle of the dance, and as you find that centeredness within yourself in a **yoga practice**, may this be a reminder for you to still **keep dancing.**

Chapter 19 — Chanting, Music, and Vibration

Chanting connects us to sound, vibration, and a way to **generate and move energy** through the body, **without requiring much physical energy**.

Our breath is a primary vehicle for moving energy, and this is why breathing exercises and generally taking deep breaths are so potent for bringing us into a deeper state of relaxation and awareness. **Singing or chanting** connects us to that **flow of energy**, regardless of what we're singing for the most part.

If we're focused on the lyrics or mood of a song, we can be aware of the state of consciousness that the song is bringing about, and by connecting to our inner heart, we can **choose music that connects more deeply with us**.

With chanting, oftentimes chants are songs of devotion, or ways to **wake up the heart** to the meaning of life, and words are repeated in a way where we're using our voice as a means of **offering up** of our problems and our joys, the good and the bad, it's all getting offered up.

With chanting, everything we have is being offered through our voice, and it's a way of **burning through anything that's holding us back**, as well as **elevating the positive** things within us, and that's a deeper take on it, but that's **true to music** in many ways.

The power of music is within each one of us, it's our ability to dance through life, to highlight the things that matter, and to burn through the things that we don't need to hold on to.

Chanting, because it's often times repeated, even something as simple as **chanting "om" over and over** again, becomes about more than just connecting to song lyrics or even making the voice sounding good in the first place, it's more about **the**

exercise, the feeling, and the will to connect to that principle of vibration and resonance.

In many cultures, there's the understanding that there are profound benefits to chanting. Even **2500 years ago, Pythagoras knew that chanting vibrated the cerebrospinal fluid** and and even the outer layers of the skull or the layers of the skull between the actual gray matter of the brain and the skull itself gets vibrated in a way to **increase circulation in the brain.** There's benefits that have been known for a long time of **the** *intonation* **of sounds, or humming.**

As we connect music and our ability to make sounds, to its **effect on the brain and body, the way we think and feel,** it allows us to feel the **mystical nature** of what chanting can do and what we're capable of, and brings us closer to the **global musical heritage of our ancestors**.

Chanting doesn't have to be **connected to a lineage** or tradition that you're unfamiliar with, and it just as much can be a way to connect in with **many different traditions** all at the same time, whether you're **religious or not,** there's a place for singing and for music and in connection with finding that **space for silence and going within.**

Chapter 20 — Picking a Mantra, Riding a Wave

In the 1970s, people made a big deal out of what your *mantra* is or **picking your mantra,** and you're not supposed to share your mantra, and there's a certain place for mantra in life, whether you have **received it from a teacher**, or you have simply found it through some other way and you feel like it **resonates with you.**

A mantra can be something with a **strong significance** that you chant, that you sing out loud or that you say. Oftentimes, it's also mainly something that you **repeat internally**.

There's this concept of *japa,* or repetition, where *japa mantra* means **repeating a mantra throughout the day** when you're performing your tasks, and it's a way to remind you to release thinking patterns and to **go deeper into focusing** on the experience of whatever you're doing, and also as a means for **transcending the surface levels of "doing" and going into "being."**

Many traditions that came to the west from India brought that concept of a mantra, and many Westerners picked up that concept. Now it has its own cultural meaning in the West, and **for repeating a mantra to work over time**, it's something about it that we need to feel connected to deeply within ourselves.

If you're simply repeating this phrase, and whether it's in another **language like *Sanskrit* or in English** or whatever your language is, this can be a way to **find meaning through simplicity**.

Many **affirmations are similar to mantras,** you can repeat throughout the day like "I am a source of infinite love" or "I am a match for success." Whatever the affirmation is, you have to find that **meaning backed by a strong feeling within you.**

Affirmations and mantras, are variations of the same concept. One key difference is that you can change **affirmations to suit the situation**, and have a lot more variety and create your own as needed, whereas mantras are often fewer, and better to **repeat the same one** day after day, **year after year.**

The *Sanskrit mantras* are different, in that Sanskrit has been around for **thousands of years**, and it's a primordial language that goes beyond the written word. **The science of Sanskrit** is connected to the resonance of different **areas of the body**, and like music or any other vibratory science, that has a deep theory to it, just as much as an artistic expression.

Sanskrit is a **music of spoken language,** and this is why many people choose Sanskrit mantras because they feel something about them, that they may feel differently about than their own **native tongue**.

I'll share a few Sanskrit mantras, these are phrases that you can repeat at different times. The first one is *loka samastha sukhino bhavantu*, this means **may all beings be happy and free**.

Another one is *om namah shivaya,* it literally means "praise be to Shiva," *Shiva* being a representation of the aspect of God that leads to the destruction of "all things that do not serve" and the **return to the original state of being of oneness of joy,** of total surrender into that. This can be a very powerful mantra for our present day and age.

Finally, "om" as a simple reminder, just om, **repeating om.** This is a way to connect to the principle of the **vibration of creation**, this primordial vibration, which science would say is energy, and as Einstein would say $E=mc2$, we know that **all matter is energy**, and even with **quantum physics**, that subatomic particles are **vibrating waves**.

As we connect to this feeling of all of matter really as these vibrating waves, then we connect to **all of matter as a principle of sound,** and this brings us into a deeper understanding of **reality as a dreamlike wave** that we are all riding on.

Chapter 21 — Neuroscience, Ancient Wisdom of the Spine and Brain

In this day and age, when it comes to understanding more about life and ourselves, we often **turn to the lens of science for a deeper understanding of things that have been tried and tested over millennia**. Now we're starting to take apart the underpinnings of our conscious experience, and break them down into terms of **neuroscience** or **biochemistry** or **psychological** terms.

In this process, there's a **holistic approach** that we have to take at the same time while we use the lens of science. Empirical science, **the scientific method**, is inherently *reductionistic*, and at the same time, can show us a lot about the way the world works beyond the physical, when we **put the pieces back together.**

Today there's a lot of new exciting research being done on what's called **cerebrospinal fluid (CSF)**, this is the fluid that is central to the nervous system, **the spine and brain**. In cultures and traditions around the world, there are different practices that work on using this cerebrospinal fluid.

We're always using cerebrospinal fluid, and it is something that's **inherent to the biological functioning of a human being** and it's also **central to many spiritual practices**.

As we develop a deeper scientific understanding of what cerebrospinal fluid is and what it does, we can understand **spiritual practices in a scientific way,** so we can relate our understanding of things that are presented in scientific terms back to their, say, historical or spiritual roots in various traditions.

As an example, there's a lot of different yoga and breathing practices that work on moving the cerebrospinal fluid in the body. A lot of these practices you might consider forms of *kundalini yoga*, one of the most common or popular terms, but this concept of the **energy in the spine** awakening and rising up through the higher centers of the body into the brain is **common to many traditions around the world**.

When we understand that the basis of every religion or spiritual teaching is all centered in the self, in the individual, and **the individual's manifestation of consciousness as it relates to the whole**, to all of humanity or the world at large, we understand that **every practice** or every tradition at some level is ultimately is going to be about us **interfacing with the body and the nervous system** especially.

The purpose of the cerebrospinal fluid essentially is **to give life energy** to the body and mind, and give life to us in a very profound way, and the cerebrospinal fluid essentially is this like central sort of luge, this **life force that is so incredibly dense** and it plays a role in in the **functioning of the cells of the body** and in the process of awakening or moving this cerebrospinal fluid, in understanding how it moves, we can develop a greater sensitivity and awareness to these more **ecstatic states** or these states of deep presence or deep bliss, peace, joy, love, those sorts of things and have a **scientific process** of awakening.

As we develop the scientific perspective around cerebrospinal fluid, we can understand its role that it plays in traditions, where they're not specifically talking about cerebrospinal fluid and yet that's what these practices are relating to in **the body and brain.**

As an example, there are very specific breathing exercises specifically with *Kriya yoga* or different more advanced forms of yoga, **other than** Kundalini, where there is a more **gentle approach** to raising this energy and directly **working with the energy in the spine and brain,** and understanding how our breath and our cerebrospinal fluid are connected is a very important component to realize in practice.

We understand that cerebrospinal fluid is produced in the spine, it **"turns over"** about three to four times a day, from **the tailbone up to the brain and back again,** and this process of the energy rising and then falling back down again is a **natural occurrence happening in all of us every day** and at the same time when we have that conscious control of it we can use it to bring our awareness to these higher centers **in the brain to generate energy.**

The cerebrospinal fluid flows in a **hollow tube in center of the spinal column**. To describe this in yoga terms, you'd call it *shushumna*, the central **pillar of light** in the body.

In medical terms, if you picture one of the medical symbols, the *caduceus*, a staff with two snakes weaving around it, each snake representing the **parasympathetic and sympathetic nervous system**, with wings on top and the central circle point on top, representing the mind's eye, this is the same representation of the Indian concept of the *chakras*, or **energy centers**, a representation of the nervous system, **the spine and brain.** At each point where the snakes cross up along the staff, that's represents where each energy center is located, corresponding to **the largest bundles of nerve *ganglia* in the spine.**

When we understand that the two snakes are representative, according to Mauro Zapatera at Harvard Medical School, of **the pituitary and the pineal gland**, the **master hormone regulators** in the body, we can have a deeper appreciation for the ancient concept of chakras and and **the science of yoga, especially breathing and meditation, as it relates to modern neuroscience.**

In practical terms, what it means for us in terms of **"why we do a practice"** or about the greater understanding of how the process of awakening works, where it can be still **presented in any setting**, secular or religious or spiritual, and given its its appropriate place, so that we understand **what we're doing and why.**

There's this deepening understanding of how to bring the cerebrospinal fluid up from the base of the spine into **"the third eye,"** generally **the**

prefrontal cortex, this central point between the eyebrows, called "the cave of Brahma" or the "Christ consciousness center."

In neuroscience terms, the prefrontal cortex is the **most evolved part of the human brain**, which is the most evolved brain in the universe that we know of so far. The cerebrospinal fluid is **the fuel for the brain**.

The process of awakening the cerebral spinal fluid and is essentially **living in harmony** with nature, living in harmony with yourself and the laws of the universe. Over time we develop a greater understanding of what that is and how to have integrity in ourselves and grow our connection or our **awareness of our biological functions** so that we can be of greater service to ourselves and therefore to the world.

In moving the cerebral spinal fluid, **healthy diet, healthy exercise, and proper sleep** are going to be nurturing for the cerebral spinal fluid. On top of that, in certain traditions like *Ayurveda,* the Indian medical science, Dr. Vasant Lad talks about

certain herbs can help **purify the blood and the nervous system.**

Cerebrospinal fluid has been measured to **perceive and emit light**, as we understand that this is something that is new to science in many ways, in terms of how people are understanding what it is, it's something that people have been experiencing for thousands of years in in **states of ecstatic bliss.**

We can develop a greater **perspective, connection, and awareness of our own biology** and then have **practices that cater to that** and this already exists in many of the ancient traditions of the world, but having the awareness come together so that there's one understanding like in Aldous Huxley's book called *The Perennial Philosophy*.

It's like all these **different rays of light of the Sun** are all manifested as different **philosophies or religions**, they all point back to the **same central source.**

Anything we do with **science or spirituality**, that **if it's a true thing**, it's all going to point back to the same source. Connecting to that sense within ourselves, we can see how it manifests in the world, and how we can be more connected to that flow within ourselves.

The cerebrospinal fluid has a **resonant field, the center point being in the heart**. As the heart calms down, and as the breath stills, the ultimate sort of point of stillness is the **state of breathlessness**, and as as we reach breathlessness, then the cerebrospinal fluid reaches maximum flow and begins to move from the brain back into the heart, as the this high consciousness, this **substance of pure awareness** reaches and **flows into the heart**, and flows into the body, that's when we experience these deeper states of **bliss**, called *samadhi*.

Samadhi, in Patanjali's *Yoga Sutras,* the foundational text of yoga practice, is the eighth limb or the highest state of being, that is this union with God, atonement, Self-realization, is the the goal of yoga. The union with all, the **state of oneness**, is a this is a real experience, a very direct experience, that we all are capable of having, and even **yearn for unknowingly**. It's not just for a select few, and it's a matter of **demystifying it so it's more accessible** in modern terms.

Cerebrospinal fluid is central to **spiritual traditions as well as neuroscience**, it was known in in ancient times around the world, and the neuroanatomy of the brain is **not a modern concept**, but the **amount of detail that we have now** is much greater.

In recognizing we're all here on the same planet, all trying to figure out the same thing, and we want to understand and **communicate with each other,** science can be one lens for that. Cerebrospinal fluid has this deep connection to many ancient traditions, and at the same time it's something that's just now being explored and **measured in the lab** in a rigorous way.

It's great to share knowledge where you can **directly interface with your biology and energy**, and get a better sense of how this energy and this fluid moves in your body, and by developing a greater sensitivity and awareness to that, we can find those states of bliss, **to feel the power of peace, joy, and love** in our hearts and in our lives. That's **why we're here**, and I'm grateful that you are here, to be able to share this with you, for you to experience and **experiment**, and **make decisions according to your experience**.

—

As for the **benefits of meditation**, approach it from the angle that everything you need is **all built-in**, the body-mind is the vehicle for practice through breath, feeling, and awareness. This **positive-feedback loop** aids you in being well, **getting to the root** of suffering, learning what you really need to thrive.

Studies on meditation indicate where significant changes occur in the brain with repeated practice:
• increased volume in the prefrontal cortex (the center of awareness, concentration and decision-making)

• increased grey matter and cortical folds (capacity for emotion and thinking)
• thicker corpus callosum (bridge of neurons connecting left "analytical" and right "creative" hemispheres)
• maintaining health of myelin sheath with age (protecting neurons)
• reduced activity in the deep brain's limbic system (fear, anxiety, stress center)
• reduced activity in the "default mode network" (DMN), the ruminating "me" center
• increasing the size of the hippocampus (memory and learning center)
• more whole-brain connectivity, especially in regions of emotion and self-regulation
While this this research is validated with neuroscience, it correlates to people's positive experiences of improved well-being matching their brain scans.

When researchers put electrodes on monks heads, **the monks laugh and point to the heart**, because they know something science is just starting to understand, the heart is responsible for feeling, without heart, the brain means nothing. In some Eastern languages, **the word for mind and heart are the same**. Remember the Beatles, "all you need is love."

Chapter 22 — Einstein and The Science of Light (*Autobiography of Yogi*)

At some point in time **before recorded history,** we started using language, words. We began communicating **vibrations through sound waves** that we carried information on, to pass on to each other.

We developed over time more evolved and nuanced **forms of communication** through language, and over time we structured these forms of language into various disciplines, **realms of knowledge and self-expression.**

And as we stand at the precipice of this new advent in language, the augmentation of **natural language processing by machines,** we still understand the fundamental mystery of our place in the world in creation and the role that the

ancient technology of language that has been with us for so many thousands of years is the primary vehicle of our **consciousness development** as well as **technological innovation**.

In this following excerpt from *Autobigraphy of a Yogi*, written at the time of the invention of the atomic bomb, **Yogananda shares revelations in quantum physics** from friends like **Albert Einstein** about the **science of light**, atoms, waves, and the **nature of this universe:**

Among the **trillion mysteries of the cosmos**, the most phenomenal is light.

Unlike sound waves, whose transmission requires air or other material media, light waves pass freely through the **vacuum of interstellar space.**

Light remains the most subtle, the **freest from material dependence** of any natural manifestation. **Einstein's velocity of light**, 186,000 miles per second, dominates the whole **theory of relativity.**

Einstein proves mathematically that the velocity of light is, so far as man's finite mind is concerned, **the only constant in a universe of unstable flux.**

On the sole absolute of light velocity, depend **all human standards of time and space**, not abstractly eternal as previously considered.

Time and space are relative and finite factors, deriving their measurement validity only in reference to the yardstick of light velocity. In joining space as a dimensional relativity, **time has surrendered age-old claims to a changeless value.**

Time is now stripped to its rightful nature, a simple essence of ambiguity. With a few equational strokes of his pen, **Einstein banished from the cosmos every fixed reality except that of light.**

In his **unified field theory**, the great physicist embodies in **one mathematical formula** the laws of gravitation and of electromagnetism, reducing the cosmical structure to variations on a **single law**.

Einstein reaches across the ages to the *rishis* of India who proclaimed a sole texture of creation, that of an illusion.

On this **theory of relativity**, mathematical possibilities have arisen of exploring the ultimate atom. Scientists are now asserting that not only that **the atom is energy, rather than matter,** but that atomic energy is essentially **"mind-stuff."**

The frank realization that **physical science is concerned with a world of shadows** is one of the most significant advances, Sir Arthur Stanley Eddington writes in *The Nature of the Physical World,* "in the world of physics, we watch a shadow performance of **the drama of familiar life.** The shadow of my elbow rests on the shadow table as the shadow ink flows over the shadow paper. **It is all symbolic, and as a symbol, the physicist leaves it.** Then comes **the alchemist** mind who transmutes the symbols, to put the conclusion crudely, **"the stuff of the world is mind-stuff."**

The external world has become a world of shadows. In **removing our illusions**, we have removed the substance, for indeed we have seen that that substance is one of the greatest of our illusions.

With the discovery of **the electron microscope** came definite proof of the **light essence of atoms** and of the inescapable **duality of nature.**

The New York Times gave the following report of a **demonstration of the electron microscope**, "**the crystalline structure** of tungsten, showing nine atoms in their correct positions in the space lattice, a cube, with one atom in each corner and one in the center. The **atoms in the crystal lattice** of the tungsten appeared on the fluorescent screen as points of light, arranged in geometric pattern. Against their **crystal cube of light** the bombarding molecules of air could be observed as dancing points of light, similar to **points of sunlight shimmering on moving waters."**

The principle of the electron microscope was first discovered in 1927 at the **Bell Laboratories** in

New York City, who found that the **electron had a "dual personality"** partaking of the characteristic of both a **particle and a wave.**

For his discovery of the Dr. Jekyll and Mr. Hyde quality of the electron, **"the particle-wave,"** which corroborated the prediction made in 1924 by de Broglie, French Nobel Prize-winning physicist, and showed that the entire realm of **physical nature has a dual personality**, Dr. Davison also received the **Nobel Prize in Physics.**

The universe begins to look **more like a great thought than like a great machine.** Science is now sounding like a page from the ancient Hindu *Vedas*. **From science** then, if it must be so, let man learn **the philosophic truth that there is no material universe.** Its mirages of reality all break down under analysis.

As one by one, the reassuring props of a physical cosmos crash beneath him, man dimly perceives his idolatrous reliance, his past transgression of the divine command, **"thou shalt have no other gods before me."**

In his famous equation outlining the equivalence of mass and energy, Einstein proved that the **energy in any particle of matter** is equal to its mass or weight multiplied by the square of the velocity of light. The **release of these atomic energies**, is brought about through the annihilation of the material particles. **The death of matter** has been the **birth of an atomic age of energy.**

Chapter 23 — Taking a Practice with You, Accepting Others

With all of this practice, remember that while it's important to take yourself seriously, it's also important to **not take yourself too seriously.**

Remember that **life is too short to get caught up in the differences** or in the seeming differences on the surface of various practices and traditions. We are all **more similar than different.**

To remember that **everybody's a human being,** so if one person has a different practice, that that's okay.

To **practice understanding and compassion** for all beings, whether someone is this or that, more advanced or less advanced, it's all a continuum of **opportunity for us** to show compassion and to

bring more insight to our own awareness and to our own experience.

Being **present to the feelings** that we have about our own practice, and about others, that we can share, to some degree, with people who are practicing the same thing, and also understanding that because everybody has so many **different beliefs and ideologies**, it's important to be kind and also be smart about who you choose to share with.

When you choose to share and how you choose to share, remembering that if you do **feel like you have something to share**, then the right people will find you and will come to you, and that you are a unique being with unique gifts and that **meditation can be a way to expand and explore those gifts**.

Your ability to share your gifts and in many ways **the art of making a living and the art of living** in general is very much connected to this process of awakening to ourselves and to what we'll call *dharma* or this **eternal truth or eternal**

teaching that is set up as the **unique lessons for us to learn** in this lifetime.

This is a bigger understanding, that while there is a lot of difference we can see on the surface, that looking deeper, we can see that everybody is learning how to **move towards love** and happiness. In the long arc of time, **the world does bend towards love** and compassion and truth and beauty. Being aware of this can help us bring more optimism, more **light into dark situations** and to live lightly in general, to find that space for **laughter, joy, empathy, forgiveness, and gratitude for life.**

As we connect deeper within ourselves, we find more **space for holding all of that**, for holding feeling and for releasing feeling, and for being a space where **others feel safe and secure and capable of doing the same.**

Chapter 24 — Gratitude and Re-Schooling of the Heart

I'm grateful for today, for friendship, and grateful to remember to be grateful for today. **The practice of gratitude** connects us into a **higher reality** that we're aware of that's already present.

It's looking to see the **brighter side of life** and knowing how to maintain that cheery disposition in harder situations.

There's a great blessing that one brings to being able to **change one's own situation**, and the situation around them, through maintaining that gratitude and peaceful disposition.

A positive attitude that we can look and see how positive psychology has made a name for itself in terms of the science of happiness and **optimal well-being** for people who are already well and looking to be healthier as well as **addressing mental health**.

The opportunity that we have that each one of us has to **change our own energy**, to change our perspective, to change our attitude, to change our mind, to let our heart **be open to receiving the feeling that we are full, satisfied, content.**

The paradox is that we empty ourselves at the same time, that there's the **refilling of the empty cup** which is infinitely refilled.

There's an ample-ness of space to hold the **infiniteness of energy**, life, and light that we are.

As we recognize our own cosmic roots and connection to **what makes us happy**, the more that we focus on those things, the more that we experience them, and the more we create a **field of positive energy** which we can then spark others to do the same.

Our own light cannot be diminished by others' light. As we witness each other shining brighter, there's the brilliance like **stars in the sky,** rather than it being about the brightest star in the sky. You can imagine us as stars all rooting for each other, "shine, shine shine!" Everybody next to each other is saying, **"come on, you can do it!"**

As we bring our **energy and focus into the day** to receive with gratitude the blessings of our cosmic home, we awaken in oneness when we see in the **grand expanse of space and time**, **the miracle** that we're existing here and now at all.

Here and now is eternal, and it's always the present moment, so even space and time have a way of showing us that we are connected to **this grand play**, playing out over the arc of eons of time, where we're playing a **small and yet somehow very significant** part in the whole thing. Our part is a reflection of the whole that **we are who we need to see in the world.**

That there's a space for you to be that person that you need to see in the world. That's why we're here, to be everything that you can, **everything that you are**.

To be yourself, and to know that your **self is beyond your personal identity** and that the Self (big S) is reflected in all people. It's that **common ground of awareness** that we all share just walking along the street, waving and saying hi to people that you've never seen in your life before. It's that shared collective awareness or consciousness.

And expanding into that, that space of expanded individuality. That you are **beyond the body and thoughts,** aware of **the breath and pure feeling.**

The breath is an expansive **doorway into interconnectedness** or interbeing, the interrelatedness that we all share with life, when there's a tree next to you that's exhaling oxygen, and **you're breathing the breath of a tree.** You're in an interconnected relationship with a tree or with a forest.

The same goes for the entire **web of life**, though the more we understand the relationship of a bacteria, to a fungus, to an insect, to a tree, we can see how soil is created and feeds the being which creates oxygen for us to breathe that is requiring a **chain of life or creatures, sentient beings, all the way up to humans.**

This idea extends from beings much smaller than us to beings larger than us, a tree being something that is a **quintessential reminder of our connection to nature**, that it's something that is larger than a human, yet still capable of awareness. Trees have brought us a **sense of home** for a very long time.

When we reflect on taking a breath, letting go of the body and letting go of the thoughts, then we can feel ourselves moving into this **state of inter-being,** with something as simple as understanding our connection to a tree and the ecosystem or web of life all around us.

The people around us too, these connections or **relationships are fractals** and our experiences are opportunities for us to learn how to grow and **learn the lesson** that needs to be learned and move on to the next lesson.

Through **trials and teachings**, we gain perspective or perception and awareness and recognize the temporariness of human life and yet it's eternal lessons, from the **cosmic perspective**.

When **we remember** that deeper nature of interbeing of our eternal self, and the self of being yourself or who you are **beyond the limited identity of who you "think" you are.**

We have a great deal of **filtering mechanisms placed on everyday thinking** so that we can be aware of the world and do the things that we have to do like brush our teeth, take care of our lives. In the same way, the electromagnetic spectrum of light, emits only 0.0001% *visible* light that we see, so **99.9999% of the electromagnetic spectrum is invisible**, x-rays, ultraviolet rays, infrared, that, even sound frequencies, radio waves, etc. **So it is with the nature of who we are, seeing beyond the surface takes practice.**

We can see visible light, and if we only **saw the world the way an ant sees, or a bird sees, or**

a bee sees, or a dolphin sees, in the same way this it would give us a different **lens of perception,** so **inner practices** give us a way to **develop a greater sense of inner sight.**

Taking this bird's eye view perspective lets us begin to **see through the eyes of another.** When we go deep enough into this we see ourselves through the other or that we **see ourselves reflected in the other,** as somehow an extension of us.

When we wear socks to keep our feet warm, the **socks become an extension of us** and when we are aware of it, we think of them as softness attached to our feet during the day. It's like the experience of being aware of what it's like **to be connected and still defined in your energy.**

That there's the **awareness of the identity of the body and the thoughts** on some level, and then we acknowledge there's **another level of awareness that's unspeakable.** In doing so, we learn to speak **from the heart**, and have fun to telling stories, and sharing ideas and metaphors and ways of relating, changing perspective.

We have that capacity within us to **develop the mind's eye** or the capacity for greater awareness, perception, consciousness. All of that comes to energy and as we grow in energy as we become **more aware of our energetic nature**. The shift in awareness that happens.

Let's change our reality. **Let's let go of the unnecessary constructs that we impose on ourselves,** or be able to at least see what those constructs are more clearly. **Take a systems check on the programs.** It's helpful to **un-learn and re-learn**, or just learn the right way if we never learned in the first place.

That's all that needs to happen for now, a little **re-schooling of the heart.** Thank you.

Chapter 25 — Conclusion, Thank You for Participating

Thank you all for being part of this experience. Thank you for contributing your energy to **uplifting the consciousness of the planet,** for connecting to something deeper within yourself, to finding space to explore that.

Let's remember to **keep it simple.**

Just like with three deep breaths, **we find our center**, breathing in and out, in and out, in and out. As we choose to move forward in life, we can let down our loads and **carry the responsibilities we do have with a smile, an open heart.**

As we bring joy into every moment, we find that mirrored back to us, connecting to what it is that life is really for, **why we're here**, where we come from, where we're going, remembering that enjoying **life is something to be shared**.

And as we bring our attention to the present moment, we can always find **something to be grateful for.** We can always find space to take deep breaths and to remember that we're not alone, that this world is here to **treat people as friends**, that you never know who's a stranger who will become your friend.

Approaching life in this way, we find **great strength** in the ability to move through every experience **with skill and with a smile**. May you be blessed today and always.

Made in the USA
Columbia, SC
14 November 2024

46087890R00083